MW00571922

Praise for Donna Ashworth

'Absolutely beautiful ... Whenever I'm feeling lost, I reach for Donna Ashworth's words and feel found'
Bryony Gordon

'Beautiful and uplifting'
Davina McCall

'Powerful and comforting ... Donna's words could change your life'
Dawn French

'If there is a god Donna is doing her or his work'
Robbie Williams

'Some people have the Bible by their bed. Others a self-help manual. I have Donna Ashworth'
Susannah Constantine

'So inspiring, so heartfelt ... the way Donna writes is beyond beautiful'
Lisa Snowdon

'Soul-nurturing permission to relax, connect and be kinder to ourselves'
Fearne Cotton

'A little corner of calm within life's storm – wonderful'
Cat Deeley

‘Donna’s words are never just words, they are teachings. Provoking and inspiring, comforting and loving, I couldn’t live without them’

Kellie Bright

‘Donna’s much-needed words will no doubt empower and lift our young people today’

Lisa Faulkner

‘Like a warm hug. Donna’s words are comfort for the soul’

Tamzin Outhwaite

‘Donna is a true wordsmith. Her writings never fail to move me’

Nadia Sawalha

‘Donna has a rare gift of being able to put into words how we all feel. Her writing is like a hug from a wise friend’

Samia Longchambon

Growing Brave

Also by Donna Ashworth:

To the Women

The Right Words

I Wish I Knew

Life

Love

Loss

Wild Hope

DONNA ASHWORTH

Growing Brave

Black&White

First published in the UK in 2024 by Black & White Publishing
An imprint of Black & White Publishing Group
A Bonnier Books UK company
4th Floor, Victoria House, Bloomsbury Square, London, WC1B 4DA
Owned by Bonnier Books, Sveavägen 56, Stockholm, Sweden

Hardback ISBN: 978-1-7853-0518-4
eBook ISBN: 978-1-7853-0519-1
Audio ISBN: 978-1-7853-0761-4

A CIP catalogue record for this book is available from the British Library.

Typeset by Envy Design Ltd
Printed and bound in Great Britain by Clays Ltd, Elcograf S.p.A

1 3 5 7 9 10 8 6 4 2

Black & White Publishing is an imprint of Bonnier Books UK
www.bonnierbooks.co.uk

I dedicate this book to my followers
who have received me with a safety
net of solidarity and sisterhood.
It emboldens me no end.

“

I recommend opening a page at random each day. Somehow the book seems to know the message you need to read.

”

AUTHOR'S NOTE

My focus word for the past year was *brave*.

I believe in the power of allocating a word each January.

There is much noise fighting for our ears at the start of a new year and so, for me, drowning it all out and focusing on one thing works wonders for my peace. Since life came calling in a rather terrifying way, *brave* was the word I chose. Or perhaps it chose me?

Hope had been my focus for some time, reflecting on the happenings of 2020 and how we all endured. What it means, how it is created, stored safely, shared … and so came about *Wild Hope*, a book which was received with such love by you all. Please know, my gratitude more than matches your supportive energy.

And now, my life flows on as life will, and I have much to share with you about this five-letter word, *brave*. What it is, what it isn't and how we harness it. Is it intrinsic or can it be taught? Is it contagious and fleeting, like joy, or cultivated carefully, like faith?

In this book you will also find my learnings, my thoughts, my tools and a whole host of other soul messages that rose up along the way.

It is brave of you, truly, to open these pages, because deep down you already know there will be tears. There will be many waves of emotion and new perspectives you won't be able to leave behind.

And yet here you are.
Come in, my friends, come in.
Rest here awhile with me. We have much to unpack.

CONTENTS

Author's note ix

Where Brave Begins 1
Brave 3
Letting Light Flood In 5
I Want to Listen 9
You'll Be Okay 11
You Just Grew 13
Endless Summers 15
How to Be Brave 17
This Sorrow 21
Whose Turn Is It Next 23
Give Up 25
Flames 29
The Stars Called You Home 31
The Shape of You 33
Ode to the Sensitive 34
Stationery Shop 37
The Letters Unsent 39
Run Dark Like Me 40
Friendship Garden 45
Beyond So 47

Fear Is Not Honest 49
Angels 51
Anxiety and Me 52
You Look Great 55
Look Up 57
Nesting Dolls 61
Still You 63
Anger and Passion 65
Call Them Close 66
One Day You Will See 69
Eclipse the Sky 70
Everything 73
The Taker of the Photo 75
Tired 79
Grateful Tears 80
Melancholy 83
I Wish You Beauty 85
Life Without Your Mum 87
Warm Breeze 89
I Want to Wear Out 90
Comfort Zones 95
Introvert or Extrovert 96
Junk Drawer 99
Love at First Sight 101
Friend Ship 103
Afraid 105
Sadness Comes 106
Your Goodness 111
Always There 113
Mother, Tigress, River 115
Sad Tale 117
Search the Night 118
Soul Garden 121
The Gift 122

Paw Print on Your Heart 127
The Grief That Is Not Ours 129
Fire-Breathing Dragons 130
Mosaic 133
They Mother 135
Regenerating 137
Women Who Knew 139
The Sun Sets 141
Sacred Place 145
The Comparing 147
Yellow 149
Brave to Age 151
Ozone 153
Wildflower 155
All That Time 159
Nightlight 160
Very Best Start 163
This Platonic Song 165
Looking Away 167
Trying to Be Good 169
A Life Around 170
Zoom In 173
The Positivity Pact 175
Star-Sharing Friend 177
Hear Them 179
Joy Comes Back 181
Racing 183
Stay 185
Exhale 187
Crack On 191
Growing in Moonlight 193
Stitched 195
Kite in the Wind 197
On Time 199

Easily Pleased 201
Happy Stay-at-Homer 203
Courage to Create 207
A Hopefulist 209
Moonbeams 211
Every Little Thing 213
All the Mondays 215
A Braver You 217
Butter-Side Down 221
Came, to Pass 222
Inside a Child's Heart 225
Gather Nuts 226
Beauty Muted 229
Let Them See 231
Seeds 233
You Crossed My Mind 237
A Piece of Their Soul 239
A New Version of You 240
Save Yourself 243
Choose Your Scary 244
Orchestra 249
Winds of Change 250
Borrow Your Brave 253
Looking For Something Beautiful 255
Left You Not 257
The Unexpected Friend 259
Special 262
Inner Child 265
Wish You Courage 266
Ask the Ocean 271
Algorithms 273
Let's Talk 274
Show and Tell 279
Your Ugly 281

A Great Teacher 283
With All That Wildness 284
She Sent 287
Bruise 289
The Meaning of Life 290
Grief Is Not a Place 295
Courage Steps Out 297
Coffee With the Universe 299
Belong 301
Bravery Lives 302
Tell the Others 307
Will Be Brave 308
Forever Days 311
Growing Brave 313

Afterword 315
Acknowledgements 317
About the Author 319

WHERE BRAVE BEGINS

In childhood, it is simple
when *loved* we are brave
when love is absent, we are *afraid*

in teenage years, it is black and white
we are brave when we feel held tight
but when left to fly without a net
we are reckless
or riddled with fear
each story as sad as the other to hear

in adulthood, things get complicated

we are brave (*so brave*) for others
we got that courage from our mothers, and fathers
but we lack that childlike bravery for *self*

as though we swapped it for adulthood
maybe if we understood
that life is not supposed to be lived in fear
we could find that source again?

perhaps the journey back to brave
is a journey back to inner child
to push out fear and invite the *wild* back in
to remember we are of the same
all players in Mother Nature's game

so maybe brave begins, then
when we begin, again
loving what is us.

BRAVE

It is, without doubt, brave, to repeat this *living* every day. To put one foot in front of the other and *carry on*, over and over. It is, without doubt, courageous to love again, when you almost lost yourself to loss. And it is, unquestionably lion-hearted of you to keep trying, to show up, to come back, to venture into new when you have been burned many times, sweet one. People who jump off mountains are adventurous, adrenalin-seeking, thrill-riders, but you, you are **brave**. I hope you let yourself know it today, and every day you show your face to the light, when darkness is calling you back.

LETTING LIGHT FLOOD IN

It is an act of great courage
to paint or write
or create anything
from your heart

but once you start

it will be like sunshine
cracking through a boarded-up window
letting light flood in

just begin

and when the judges come to rain
their deeply held pain
on that beautiful bright window frame
you made

let them
do not dare fret them

you have much higher things to focus upon
and even after that window is long gone
your song will still play

to those who can hear beauty

and you will win
this game we are in

because you let the light flood in.

I wish you the bravery
to unstitch the suit they
wove for you and restitch
it to fit *yourself* in all
your unearthed glory.

I WANT TO LISTEN

If you ever want to talk
about the person you are missing
I want to listen, *always*
and as you do this talking
they come alive again, for me
whether I knew them or not
your love, your stories
your picture painting of them works
and the air around me fills with an energy
that is life-affirming and joyful
I can't explain the science
but I can only assure you of the effect
it's real
they are real
and if you ever want to talk about them
in that energy effusive
enthusiastic way that you do
I want to listen.

“

Wonderful new people who
shine light into your soul will come
on in, if you leave space.

”

YOU'LL BE OKAY

The one thing we know for sure, is that nothing lasts for ever. In this journey, you will grieve. You will grieve people who are still alive, as well as those who have passed on. You will grieve shattered dreams, and you will grieve versions of yourself you had to break free from. But that's okay. In this life nothing lasts for ever but with that same truth comes the knowledge that all pain will dissipate too. And great new things will emerge. Wonderful new people who shine light into your soul will come on in, if you leave space. And as long as you cry when you must, laugh when you can and love every day your little broken heart still beats, you will be okay. You will be more than okay.

YOU JUST GREW

It is brave to want to be better
braver still to understand
that you are already enough
but reaching for more is your right
you are a seed instructed by light
not a creature of the night
and if the other flowers in your field
do not support the way you grow
let them go
all they truly need to know
is that you are brave to want new
you are nature
you just grew
and that's okay
you did not come here to stay

let old leaves fall away.

ENDLESS SUMMERS

We hear so many warnings about treasuring the eighteen summers we spend with our children, but the truth is, they are always our children. And the memories keep coming – a little differently but just as precious, just as worth storing in the albums of your soul. These moments of bonding are lifelong, you just have to be ready to recognise them, because chances are they won't look like anything much at all, but oh they will fill your mothering heart. Slow down, my friends, there is no rush here. That child of yours is a child until the day you both walk another plane together, and even then, your baby they will still be.

HOW TO BE BRAVE

Love the moon, love sunrises
love jam with cheese
love everything you *like*, in fact
half measures are safe
but passion, that's *brave*

be you, so *you*
that it creates awkwardness
when others are not *them*

what begins as derision or disapproval
will magically morph into motivation
and much-needed *permission*
if you just brave it out

share your ugly truths
that's where the love lives
and nothing is more brave
than showing your soft skin
in a world that screams for armour

don't let loss stop you losing again

you are not here to *keep*
you are here to love
and to lose
and to do it all *again*
and again

as many times as you are gifted.

If being more you
pushes people away
they were never
supposed to be there.

THIS SORROW

I sometimes feel I brought this sorrow with me
from where I do not know
perhaps I channel it through my ancestors
the sorrow they were unable to free themselves of
in their time here on earth
maybe they are giving it to me to let it go?

so I do
I let the sorrow go
this sorrow that I do not know the origin of

and then, like the everlasting porridge pot
I find this sorrow back again
growing profusely of its own volition

trying to drown me from the inside out

and I swim through it
I float when I can no longer thrash

and on the next dawning sunrise
I let it go again

I sometimes feel I brought this sorrow with me
from where I do not know

it seems to be my journey
to forever take this sorrow
and forever let it go.

WHOSE TURN IT IS NEXT

It started when you bought me
that crystal to keep in my pocket
when you couldn't be by my side
you said it would be my guide
in dark alleyways and on *those* days

it will remind me, you said
of the light you see within my soul
and the many ways in which I'm whole

something it's hard for me to see alone

and I sent you the book
the one that finally convinced you to
follow your heart

when we are together
I buy the cakes, you get the tickets
and never once have we faltered
in our ebb and flow
of letting in and letting go
letting in and letting go

money experts
would look in wonder

at how our hearts
just simply remember

whose turn it is next.

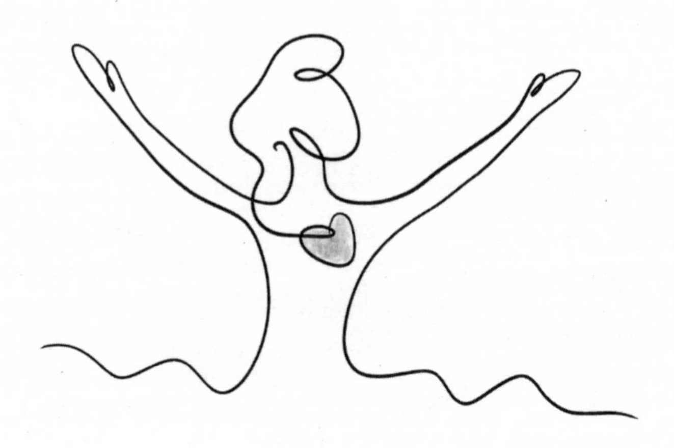

GIVE UP

Sometimes you have to give up things you really *like* to get the things you really *need*. And it's not an immediate switch, like handing ransom money to a kidnapper. There is a barren, terrifying period of nothing, where regret and familiarity plead with you to reconsider. And you have to be strong, use hope as your shield. Hope, that behind the thing you thought was great, is something much better, waiting for a clear space. Sometimes you have to give up things you like to get the things you need. And it's worth it, my friends. I promise you, it's worth it.

If you don't know how
to move forward...
just take a few brave steps
and *have faith*, the universe
will meet you there.

FLAMES

When faced with a decision that scares you, think of those who walked your lineage. The women whose bodies created line after line of your blood. The fierce females who could only dream of the opportunities you have now. Talk to your ancestors, my friend. Hear their primal roar. They are beside you, you are never alone. When faced with a risk in this life, just once or twice, jump bravely into the fire they knew so well, knowing that they will cover you, guide you through and pull you out the other side. They speak to you through your gut, these souls, with their wisdom learned in lifetimes of bravery, breakthroughs and bold beauty. Listen. Be held. And jump into the flames.

THE STARS CALLED YOU HOME

The stars have called you home, love
up high, so far away
I think they missed your brilliance
they just couldn't let you stay

you've shone that light of yours, love
on all the lives you touched
we've known your joy for years and years
I guess they thought, *enough*

they need your light up there now
this world grows ever dark
your youness will rain down like love
dripped into every heart

the stars have called you home, love
now we'll miss you, every day
and every night we'll scour the skies
to watch you where you lay

and when the clouds are gathering
and air's too cold to breathe
the life you lived will warm our bones
and your star will help us see.

“

The pain you put your body through to *fit* is exhausting, cruel and most importantly of all, pointless.

”

THE SHAPE OF YOU

It is a fool's folly to shape your body to match the trends, or someone's expectations. Trends change, expectations change, and so too do the people dishing them out. The pain you put your body through to *fit*, is exhausting, cruel and most importantly of all, pointless. It won't last, as nothing ever does. And there you will be, *perfect*, but feeling entirely worthless, used and battered, because you forgot to *feed your soul* whilst you were starving your body. Fast forward all that misery, my love, and *see*. See your body as it is. The shape of you. Unique. Flawed. So what? You didn't come here to *fit*. You came here to grow.

ODE TO THE SENSITIVE

When we fly
we soar
but when we fall
there is no floor

when we laugh
we cry
when we believe
there is no why

when we love
we *love*
we love like angels
from above

when we rage
we seethe
we feel so much
it's hard to breathe

when we care
we roar
like a thunder
from our core

when we know
we *know*
we channel light
from all that grows

when we try
we strive
the only limit
is the sky

when we fly
we soar
but when we fall
there is no floor.

STATIONERY SHOP

If you regress to childhood in a stationery shop, *I see you*. If you gather shiny journals to your chest, face alight at pastel-coloured sticky notes and to-do pads adorned with glittering foil, *I get it*. You are strong, powerful and running a world you made every day. People need you to survive. But really you are still *she*, the collector of pretty things that promise creativity and encourage your heart to channel your soul. You *do* need another journal, my friend. You really *do*. It's not something you should ever explain. It's a simple nod to that little child within, a green light for go. A *you can do this* and *we have what it takes*. Write it down with your perfect new pen. And make it so …

THE LETTERS UNSENT

So much self you have poured
into letters unsent
letters never written
except on a loop in your mind

letters seeking justice
explaining all the ways
in which you have been misread
letters written in invisible ink

all that self you poured
into these heart-wrenching pleas
when you should have been busy
penning a note to yourself
to apologise, profusely
for ever allowing the accusations
and the wrongly directed anger
to infiltrate your skin

let's begin …

Dear self, I am sorry
that I failed to protect you
once again
from somebody else's
unhealed pain.

RUN DARK LIKE ME

If you run dark, like me
you will know
that positivity takes work
that rising above the pain of this cruel planet
feels impossible sometimes
as though the weight of the deepest ocean
is pushing us down

if you run dark, like me
you will know
that letting people into your heart
knowing what damage they can do in there
is beyond brave
and yet we let them in, again and again
because love is what we do

if you run dark, like me
you will know
that daily, everyday life
so simple to so many
can feel like a marathon
a mountain climb
a trip to the ends of the earth
and back, some days

if you run dark, like me
you will know
that this life we are living is not easy
but oh it is beautiful

so beautiful in fact
that the joy it brings
can often feel like pain

if you run dark, like me
you will know
that this life will hurt
but it will also heal
the pain you brought here
from somewhere else

and the love will keep you warm
long after they go

if you run dark, like me
you will need courage
forage it and nurture it
and grow it all around

stockpile it to warm you
on days when darkness engulfs

keep that courage in your pocket

when you cannot see your way out
it will light your dark

it will light your dark.

Just begin...
the world may not
immediately embrace
your contribution but the
universe will and it's
her you need on side.

FRIENDSHIP GARDEN

In your heart there is a garden
reserved for friends
a garden to which you lovingly tend

growing beautiful flowers
whose petals will carpet
their pathway with power

and bring light
when day chills, like night

they'll be your loving shove
a universal nudge
a cosmic sign from up above

and your friends they will grow
such a garden for you
raising flowers of every height and hue
using those petals that you once threw

to make new

a never-ending give and take
such support this boundless soil will make
don't neglect it, don't forsake

what a beautiful thing
this garden creates.

BEYOND SO

It is not just rebellious
to love yourself
in a world that profits
from attacking mental health

it is courageous, *beyond* so

to refute the idea
that you are never enough
when you are already giving
so very much
when your focus should simply be
fixed on love
rise above

to shirk off the weighted cloak of shame
they handed out at the coming-of-age parade
oh this is brave
beyond so

to let yourself go
create space to overflow
let your colours finally show.

“

Fear is not always danger.
Sometimes, it is love, *remembering*
all the loss.

”

FEAR IS NOT HONEST

Fear is not honest. It is a master of disguise, in fact. In its original costume, it is easy to understand, *where there is danger, there is fear*. But over the years, as dangers became less obvious, fear became unsure and lost track of what was danger, and what was *living*. Fear became distrusting, unable to tell so readily who was a wolf in sheep's clothing and who was grandma, in need of soup. And I suppose, in a roundabout way, what I am trying to say is, don't always believe the fear you feel. Pick it up, give it a closer look, undo its wrapping and see what skin it hides. Fear is not always danger. Sometimes, it is love, *remembering* all the loss. Give it a hug and some soup, and off you go.

ANGELS

I like to think angels pull souls from bodies
before pain and tragedy strike

safe from harm in loving arms

pressing eyes and ears against soft wing
so they know no earthly suffering

only love, only safety, only peace
I think, no matter how they leave

they are protected as they go

and whilst this act I cannot prove
just like I can't explain to you
the invisible power of hope or love
or the magic of seeking solace in beliefs

I feel it makes some sense of grief

just like I feel
no, I know, that it's real

that people live on
never leaving us alone

long after the angels
lift us up and take us home.

ANXIETY AND ME

I woke today with anxious thoughts
and not the usual kind
a head of buzzing locusts
trying to chew away my mind

my stomach churned with anguish
my skin too hot to touch
fear flooded every organ
my brain dissolved to mush

my breath was fast and shallow
my lungs refused to fill
my body not responding
to any medicine or pill

so I sat amidst this madness
and I let it overwhelm
tired of trying to live like this
I let go of the helm

and whilst the riot raged
and heartbeat drummed my ears
a kind of soothe came seeping in
I've lived like this for years

I met with the anxiety
and asked her to sit down
perhaps there is a better way
to turn this ship around

surprisingly, she silenced
for she'd never been addressed
as to why she causes so much dread
and thrives in such a mess

and sure enough when questioned
her bluster hid much more
some grief, some fear, some trauma
I hadn't seen before

together, we unpacked it
and cried as we revealed
the things I'd swallowed down
the pain we hadn't healed

and now when I wake *anxious*
and chaotic thoughts abound
I ask her what she's bringing up
for me to work around

we pace it out together
each feeling welcomed in
then delegated to its place
to let the peace begin

and though she won't yet leave me
and sometimes gets too loud
I'm fond of her, for all her faults
in fact, I think I'm proud.

“

When I say *you look great*, it’s your growth and your peace I am complimenting.

”

YOU LOOK GREAT

When I say *you look great,* it's not because you're in shape, or your hair looks perfect. It's because your energy is *lit*. It's literally clearing a pathway into the room for you, like a dazzling red carpet of light. Your aura is vibrating, glowing through your skin in a way that suggests you might just have been kind to yourself recently. There's an air of acceptance about you that hints: you may just be getting used to the concept that you're amazing, that you glow up every situation you walk into and the impact you have on people is one of joy. When I say *you look great*, it's your growth and your peace I am complimenting. Because I see how wonderful you are, but if you see it too, then that's worth saying. That's really worth saying.

LOOK UP

When someone so very full of light leaves
your world feels dark, I know
but that light they shone
that light of theirs
it's not out
it doesn't end
it *moves*
as though the stars themselves
plucked it from earth
and placed it proudly
amongst their constellations
to shine alongside them
forevermore
bringing hope and guidance
to the entire planet
so, when that darkness cloaks you
when their light leaves your world
I guess what I'm trying to say is
look up, my friends
look up.

You mustn't run on a broken leg
bones rest to heal, that's true
but you can still love with a
broken heart and you must
because love's the glue.

“

They were exactly who they were,
so that you could be you today.

”

NESTING DOLLS

I think every version of the woman we have been lives within us still, like those wooden nesting dolls we played with as children. And truly, we cannot begin to fully love ourselves until we take each one of those dolls out and honour them, just as they are. All the mistakes, all the flaws, all the ways in which you thought them disappointing. They were exactly who they were, so that you could be you today. And each is so beautiful, if you are bearing in mind how brave it is to try. As you make peace with these dolls, one by one, be emboldened by the knowledge that the very final shell of this creation, the very final you, will be the you you were *supposed* to be; having known, and loved, all the yous, you were supposed to be then too.

STILL YOU

It is brave to believe in the unproveable
in a world that demands fact

it is brave to keep magic in your heart
when others laugh
at the way you bottle it up to share
then readily gobble down that light
when they have none

it is brave to let yourself out of that cage
the world built around you
knowing you grew to rely
on the safety of those bars

all of this is brave
but bravest of all without doubt

is the way you love again
when someone who was once
invited into your home
burned it down around you

and you gathered up those ashes
cast them to the wind
to disperse to the universe
for whatever its will demanded

and here you are
after all you've been through
still soft as butter
still all you.

ANGER AND PASSION

Maybe you don't feel white-hot rage sometimes, for no apparent reason. I do. It zips through my limbs like sharp electric currents and roars around my rib cage like a thunderstorm in a bottle. Sometimes it feels as though this anger may eat me alive if I let it. So I take the rage, in my mind, and like whey is removed from milk, I filter the passion from the chaos of this feeling. Because that passion is important. It is the cause, the *why*, the injustice from somewhere along the way you forgot to honour or lost your courage to do so. Then, I open the window and let all that murky roaring chaos out. I bottle up the passion to hold up in front of my eyes, so I can see it, then use it as fuel to make this world a better place, even if only in the tiniest of ways.

CALL THEM CLOSE

By withholding a passed one's name
you're not protecting the grieving
from a wave of sadness

those waves are higher-ruled
like the moon and the tides

by withholding a lost one's name
you're not saving the grieving
from a sadness they had forgotten

they never forget

saying a name
does something far more powerful
than create more pain

I believe it calls them close
from where they are

I believe, it brings them
into that moment

I believe it fills the air
with an energy,
that's so very much full of *them*

I believe this act
is what it means
to be remembered
is what it means
to leave a legacy

I believe, my friends
that it keeps them with us

so be brave
call them close
and let love fill your heart.

ONE DAY YOU WILL SEE

It is only with the vision of hindsight that we see how brave our parents have been. How many times we scared them senseless, without care for their soft hearts. How they loved us *still* when our tongues lashed out like angry whips on bare skin. *One day you will see*, they said. And we do. We really do. We see it all now. The overwhelming love and fear, as newborn skin meets skin, in a world hiding danger at every twist and turn. We know it now, that angst, that constant gnawing worry, that absolute *love* that often feels so powerful, it could squeeze us to death in its vice-like grip. It is only when we are grown that we truly see who *grew* us. And if we could take back every moment of indifference and replace it with utter devotion, oh but we would. We very much would.

ECLIPSE THE SKY

I want to write but the floor is dirty
the washing is a mountain spewing heat
and the list of my failures of the week
is itching to be ticked

I want to think
all my randomly ridiculous thoughts
without interruption
but outside chat is loud and messy
and life itself just will not let me
sit with them
so my musings may soar and swoop
like geese finding their formation
and form an orderly V

I want to play
but adulthood doth disallow
and yet my inner child screams loud
and she will not take no for an answer, that one

so no, I will not work right now
when I do not know what time's allowed
to me, on this journey, of life

and if the sky will ever look again
quite as it does in this moment
I will be, today
just *be*, today

just in case, I cannot be tomorrow
what point in risking all that sorrow?
a day is only set to die
if lists rise to eclipse the sky.

EVERYTHING

What of those brave babies who were not held like precious cargo? Those children who grew tall and strong, with little light and soil too dry? Those brave souls who walk among us, wishing they had known what love looked like so long ago. I will tell you what of them; they are out there, loving *more*. Loving enough for an army, in fact. These brave, brave babies are out there, breaking chains, righting wrongs and throwing their self-taught love around, like the substance of great power it is. If you get the chance to love someone like this, my friends, love them with your all. They did not come this far to accept anything other than, *everything*.

THE TAKER OF THE PHOTO

I am the taker of the photos
I am the receiver of the groans
eye-rolls and *hurry ups*
I am the one who disrupts the *moments* to capture them
but I am also the holder of the memories

I am the holder of the stories
I am the one who keeps the precious proof
and if you are too
please know
you are capturing this life
as it happens

capturing stages, ages, twists, turns
and last moments
no one could have foreseen

generations to come
will thank you for this
even if no one does right now

the eye-rolls will be replaced one day
with absolute all-consuming gratitude
for the image of a smiling face so missed
and a memory returned home to stay

keep disrupting life to capture it
when it's all that is left
someone somewhere
will be so very glad you did.

Those who lament the
many ways you've changed
do so because they fear
they've stayed the same.

TIRED

She woke up one day *tired*, but not tired in the way more sleep can fix; tired like a tree whose roots are rotting. Tired of holding up her entire world, day after day; like Atlas, *alone,* with the burden of such blessings. Tired of running so fast, only to never keep up. Tired of giving too much, for it to never be enough. Tired of wanting all the time, tired of lacking all the time, tired of the mental load this life demands. Tired of smiling over screams of injustice, shouts of unfairness and roars of *give me more* – but not more of this; give me more of *that*. More freedom, more water, more wind in my sails and sand on my feet. More space, more time, more moments of peace and clarity, more of what happens when life is being lived and not *achieved*. That day, as she woke up, she really did wake up.

GRATEFUL TEARS

How do I say goodbye
to the sun that warms my sky
to the moon that guides the night
with its courage-giving light

how can I find the words
the thought is so absurd
like the forest full of trees
rising up to take its leave

how can I walk away
how do I face a day
that doesn't hold you in it
I won't survive a minute

but then I hear your voice
reminding me of choice
the love you brought with you
is still here, it is the glue

so special was your path
so magical, your laugh
so lucky was my chance
to hold you in this dance

and so I'll leave you here
and let you keep my fear
and love is all I'll take
the love you helped me make

sleep sweetly, safe and loved
send signs from up above
I thank you for the years
as I cry grateful tears.

MELANCHOLY

Melancholy is here again
I'm starting to think of him as friend
he comes to visit with his key
to unlock the grief inside of me
and often, though he ruins the mood
I think that deep down he is good
for to be alive is to be heartbroken
and when he comes he cracks me open
and reminds me living is all things
he reminds me, caged birds cannot sing.

I WISH YOU BEAUTY

I wish you beautiful moments
the little kind
warm drinks in cosy spaces
sunrises that breathe life into your very being
and sunsets that soothe you to sound slumber

I wish you beautiful people
the true kind
people who smile with the strength of a thousand suns
and love with the warmth of them too
people who see the privilege
in you allowing them access
to the vaults of your heart

I wish you many beautiful *hellos*
that open up new doors
to exciting worlds of adventure and healing
and parts of your soul you had closed off long ago
or never dared to journey into

I wish you beauty in this life, my friend
but most of all, I wish you the *bravery*
to see that beauty in yourself

because it is there
it is always, truly, definitely there.

LIFE WITHOUT YOUR MUM

Life without your mum means you are now *she*. You are the one who creates all that *life*. You are the one who honours the family traditions and ensures that joy, nurture and wisdom are passed down, as she would have liked. You are the one who solves all of the problems, for everyone, just as she did so beautifully for so very long. But that is hard when you are hurting, when you are still just a little girl deep down who misses her mama very much. So, be kind to that little girl but go forth and do what your mother taught you to do … *love*. Because one thing is for sure, she taught you well.

“

Happiness is a weather front
not a place.

”

WARM BREEZE

Happiness is not a constant state of being. It's a warm breeze that blows over your life in soul-stroking waves, in between all the other emotions. Happiness is a weather front, not a place. And it should come and go. Because your garden, whether you realise it or not, needs all the weathers to stay healthy. You don't become *happy*, my friends, you become content, peaceful, accepting. Which simply means, when that warm breeze of happiness blows your way, you're ready to tilt your face up – and feel it.

I WANT TO WEAR OUT

I want to wear my body out
as I was always supposed to
but only in the most beautiful of ways

how to identify the beautiful ways
amidst the shouty swathe of *buy this*
or *drink this poison to forget*

each time you tire joints climbing mountains
for views that put stars in your soul
that's a beautiful way to wear out

all the pizza shared with sullen teens
building sugar and carb bridges
to connect generations
finding gateways between hearts
to share their bonded beat
that's a beautiful way to wear out

all the sun we couldn't keep out of
because the sea and the waves
and the beauty of this earth's LIFE
was just too joyously inviting
that's a beautiful way to wear out

all the laughter, the elixir of life's joy
that creased our face
to paper-thin parchment
as ringed with life as any tree
that's a beautiful way to wear out

anything else, any quest to hit the grave
with fuel in the tank
or a shell that's so shiny for its age

is not a way
I will waste my wearing out on.

A gentle reminder
to never compare
your gloriously authentic
messy wondrousness
to somebody else's
carefully curated
online content.

COMFORT ZONES

Despite popular belief, I don't believe life is better without comfort zones. I think, in fact, that without comfort zones, life is far too terrifying to truly enjoy. But the thing about those comfort zones, is that they're not meant to be where you *live*, they're meant to be where you *rest*. Where you regenerate. If you make a home in your comfort zone, you will stay within limiting lines, never feeling the wind in your sails, the world at your feet and the rush of *life* as it whisks you off the ground and shows you the source of all that it's made of. Your comfort zone is a place you made when the world showed you its teeth. And you can go there, anytime, to remind yourself you created a sanctuary. You did that. But don't stay. It will be there when you need it. When you are temporarily done seeing the world as your brave little self.

INTROVERT OR EXTROVERT

Am I introvert or extrovert, you ask?
I am whatever
the sun is

some days I burn with fiery glare
so hot the earth reflects my flair
and other days I hide in cloud
my light no longer fierce or proud

am I introvert or extrovert, you ask?
I am whatever
the moon is

some nights I give out such a show
it's hard to slumber in my glow
yet other nights I'm but a hue
of grey amongst the inky blue

am I introvert or extrovert, you ask?
I am whatever
the ocean is

some waves I hurl upon the shore
as though they held a million more
and others barely touch the sand
like a feather drawn across your hand

am I introvert or extrovert?
I cannot truly say
it's anybody's guess
depending on the day

you may see me roar
like a tempest on the sea
or shine a summer heatwave
as though that light is free

but whatever me you get
don't assume that's who I'll stay
like nature we are seasonal
often all in just one day

am I introvert or extrovert?
this question holds a trap
like the universe, we are everything
no label speaks to that.

JUNK DRAWER

Every human has a junk drawer they simply cannot keep control of. The next time you are in paralysing awe of someone shiny or beaten down by an energy mightier than your own, remember that. Everyone plucks a stray hair from somewhere unsightly. And they go to bed with worries and fears tucked in with their duvet, just like you. Every single human has a drawer filled to burst with utter uselessness they never get around to sorting and no matter how great things appear outside-in, they wish they were better at something. Everyone has a junk drawer, a stray hair, a part of their body they hide and a relationship that collapsed because of fear and miscommunication. These things we berate ourselves for daily, may even connect us more, than the good stuff we so readily share.

LOVE AT FIRST SIGHT

I believe that love at first sight
is simply souls recognising one another

you may not have seen that person before
but oh you *know* them

somewhere inside you *knew* they existed
and you already *know* their energy
by heart

and that moment
those first eyes across a room
is less
wow, love has struck me from above
and more
there they are

so yes, I believe in love at first sight
for the mind, the eyes and the body

but your soul
    has seen them before.

“

If friendship is a ship, and friends are crew mates – then I am glad so glad, you are mine.

”

FRIEND SHIP

I like to think a friendship is just that: a ship. Some are built to last. Made to navigate any ocean, whatever the weather. Perfect for feeling the breeze in your hair, seeking exciting new adventures and seeing life at its lightest. But strong enough to navigate the changing tides, the rising storms and the roughest of hosting seas. If friendship is a ship, and friends are crew mates – then I am glad, so glad, you are mine. We built her well, this ship of ours. We built her out of laughter, loyalty and most of all, love. And she will carry us safely, I think. Right to the very end of our worldly adventures. And perhaps, I suspect, even after that.

AFRAID

You're supposed to be afraid

the human heart is desperately soft
and this world is desperately hard

it seems simple to me
of *course* you should feel afraid
how could you not?

but you're supposed to *do* this life afraid
that's the key, the *doing*

your fear is not supposed to build forts
around your heart
or fence in your *living*

your fear is only supposed to be
an alarm system
that's it
just a warning bell
not a wall

because sometimes walls keep out
more good stuff
than bad.

SADNESS COMES

Sadness came to tea last night
as she's often done before
but I didn't let her in this time
I stopped her at the door

I'm off to meet with friends, I said
your timing isn't right
I can't allow your atmosphere
it's not the place tonight

but sadness would not take the hint
her manners lack finesse
her pace was slow and heavy
yet she kept up nonetheless

and even when I took my seat
amongst my laughing friends
she squeezed herself right in between
her boldness never ends

and I was sure my friends would loathe
this spectre at the feast
and somehow think me lesser
for inviting such a beast

but no, their warmth was undeterred
as if nothing was askew
I think perhaps they know by now
I sometimes come as two

and even sadness seemed to glow
a lighter shade of grey
to know that she's accepted
seemed to lighten up her day

so let your sad accompany you
don't think her hard to share
no need to face her all alone
just pull an extra chair.

There are people in this life
who will cut you open
just to see what you are made of
show them it is *love*.

YOUR GOODNESS

When someone accuses you of an ugly deed, a part of you instantly becomes it. *I knew it*, your inner critic gloats. And perhaps you will then spiral into shame, consumed by the blame. But if all your working parts are in order, there should be a faint knock at the window of your heart right then. A knock that will grow louder, as the you you absolutely know yourself to be, is roused to defend its essence. And as your inner self rises to claim its rightful place, ego and anger will join in, inciting you to attack those who brought these claims your way. But wait all of that out. The fight outside is not yours to join. It only matters that your inner parts, your *yous*, are on side. The root of your intentions and the goodness of your heart need only be known by you. And the rest will see it, when they want to.

ALWAYS THERE

I have a friend who is always there
and she worries that her care
is not enough
that her words may be clumsy
and rough
and will not be the safety mat
I need to land

if only I could make her understand

that having a friend who simply sees me
frees me
she believes in me

and when the winds rage hard my way
it is towards this friend I wildly sway

and I have come to realise
these precious bonds are the prize

and friends are angels
in disguise.

MOTHER, TIGRESS, RIVER

A mother
inner strength, like no other
a tiger, in tigress dress
she will outrun dangers without stress
and swiftly turf them from her nest

mothers are unstoppable
in the way that rivers cease to flow
when summer suns have dried them so
yet by divine intervention waters grow

nature always finds a way

and a mother's love is built to stay

forever finding ways to say
I'm here

rivers rushing in your ears
let her bravery fight your fears.

SAD TALE

It will come to pass that your good heart will not always be taken care of. That your kind soul will not always be kept well by others. That your acts of love will be twisted into ugly stories, tales in which you are the villain. And it will hurt this good heart of yours, to hear that such mistruth exists, that there are those who will turn pure into *plots* and selfless into *subterfuge*.
But when this sadness comes about, as it must, be *brave*. You know this heart of yours and all the care it holds for our world and all in it. You know what you did not do and what you did do, so beautifully. And those who can see, *do* see you. Or they will, very soon. The others, may never be able to. And that, my friend, is a sad tale much bigger, than any they have set out to create.

SEARCH THE NIGHT

When I die
let everyone say of me whatever they will

for if I am now alive in only memory
it will be their own version of me
the one they *chose* to see

and not the me I knew
just like I will remember you
by the way you made me feel
that's what remains real

if I am to die
let my faults be held high too
uphold the truth

I grew every day I breathed
so do not be deceived by
she was sunlight
sometimes I was rain

and saying that
comes with no shame
it will help others weather
their own storms better
you see

when I die
let all my colours
fly to the stars
to find their place
no longer in the rat race
but now relegated
to perpetuate space

with more light
to burn ever bright

if you wish to hold me tight
search the starry night.

SOUL GARDEN

We know we must look after our mental health as well as our physical, but what about the other kind: our soul health? I feel there are three pillars to my wellbeing and if I am to be at peace, they must all be tended to like a garden growing a cornucopia of colourful plants. They do not all need the same things. My mental health needs focus, organisation and calm to thrive. My physical health requires fresh food, restful slumber and rivers of water. But my soul health needs laughter. It needs carefree periods where time is unmonitored and it needs connection to the source that holds us all in place. It needs to be reminded that escapism is not wandering aimlessly through forests; that act is, in fact, what we are very much supposed to be doing. My soul garden is in bloom when light is being sought and love is at the forefront of all I choose, starting with me.

THE GIFT

In the untimely event of my death
immediately unwrap everything
you have kept for new
I will enjoy it in spirit with you

take out all your brightest colours
and clash so hard
the sun will be in awe of your light
I want you alive and present
and rainbow-bright

eat cake
and slather butter on your bread
this is the prize for not being dead

book a holiday
somewhere we said we must go
walk to the forest, make it long and slow
watch everything grow

touch your face, that nose
you so often berate
marvel at how you arrived so late
to see its beauty
to see it daily now, is your duty

set your watch
time is not yours
but oh this life, it is
and it's down to you
how you choose to live
this is the gift
my dying, will give.

What of that bravery
that never gets a spotlight
the way you held till sunrise
survived your darkest night?

PAW PRINT ON YOUR HEART

If you have a paw print on your heart
you know of brave love

loving something you *know* must *go*
too soon

this best friend you found
without words or common ground
learning to speak
with cuddles and soft sounds

goes around too fast
it cannot last

yet the paw prints they leave
on our hearts stay forever
their soul like a tattoo
indelibly treasured

to do this once is to know true joy
to do this twice is to know true courage
to do it again and again and again

is to show

what brave love *is*.

“

The grief unspoken. Throbbing like
a radioactive lump in our souls.

”

THE GRIEF THAT IS NOT OURS

What of all the grief that isn't ours to grieve out?
The funerals we cannot attend but wish we could.
The people we don't even know; little faces in
newspapers or on screens, strangers who leave a
mark on our hearts as though they once lived there.
The people in high places, who shaped our lives
indelibly, without ever having known who we are.
All that grief we do not grieve because it is not *ours*.
And yet there it is. The grief unspoken. Throbbing
like a radioactive lump in our souls. Not all grief
comes from reciprocated love; sometimes it comes
from respect, gratitude, humanity, familiarity – or the
simple act of having a heart that beats and breaks.
And that's okay. If there is grief in your bones, grieve
it out, my friends. Any way you like.

FIRE-BREATHING DRAGONS

When you were little
I could wash your whole world happy
I could chase the monsters from under your bed
and fill your heart with joy
and I did, my love
oh how I did

your life was in the palm of my hands
and I kept you safe there
every day I could

and now, not so little
your world is no longer mine to paint bright
life has you in its grasp
and I can only watch and hope

that your lessons will land first time
your heartaches will blossom
into passion for *more*
and your worth will stay untouched
like a precious jewel
secreted away in a cave
beyond the bluest of seas
guarded by fire-breathing dragons of gold
and all that *magic we made*

and you, my brave, *brave* child
are the hero in this story
this tale of love that grew arms and legs
and then wings to fly away with

and I, am the ever proud narrator
who watches from afar
and gathers your chapters
to stitch into the book of my soul

it is, without doubt the biggest blessing of all
to be able to let go
of something so precious
so that something even more precious again
can breathe air

and the best thing about such love is
it never dies, *never*
when you can no longer see it
or touch it
you can still feel it

and if you need to imagine where I am
there I'll be
in our secret cave beyond the bluest of seas
guarding your worth
with the fire-breathing dragons of gold

forevermore.

MOSAIC

You are a beautiful mosaic

and even if broken apart

your coloured shards scattered around
pieces picked up from the ground
and gathered again
rearranged
to make something new

it would still be *you*

because you are not the picture that's seen
you are the colours, the in-between
you are the thread that stitches the seams
the soul that walks at night in dreams

you are the light making home from stone
you walk with an army all of your own

you are art
that part
is true

but no matter how you're rearranged
the pieces that make you

remain the same.

“

They are walking around this earth with nurture flowing out of their pores.

”

THEY MOTHER

Not all mothers are mothers. Some mothers are aunts by blood or by royal appointment. Some are sisters or best friends, with safe spaces for laps and listening ears so large they can hear silent cries. Some are teachers who will be remembered lifelong for all the right reasons. Not all mothers are mothers. And if you have one in your life, you are blessed. They have much love to give. And they are walking around this earth with nurture flowing out of their pores. Not all mothers are mothers, but oh how they *mother*. And this world should throw petals at their mothering feet, as they teach us all, how unconditional love is done.

REGENERATING

I don't think you're simply tired

I think you're regenerating

like all of Mother Nature's children in winter
whether seasonal or of the soul
your instinct is to curl up
hunker down and reset

you're not less
you're simply in tune with the sun

and as the dark days begin to wane
your inner wild fortifies and evolves
bolstered and renewed, cocoon-style

ready for the new beginnings
ready for the reinvent
ready
simply ready

let yourself be led
down the rabbit hole
when the weariness washes over
and your body begs to rest

I don't think you're simply tired
I think you're regenerating.

WOMEN WHO KNEW

I come from a long line of women who *knew*. Women who *got it*. Women who were first to heal, last to attack. Brave women who created more brave women. Brave enough to see that softness is strength, that weakness lives in the hard shells not the bare face. I come from a long line of female warriors who never picked up a sword but moved mountains with their silent cries and long-suffering bearing of unbearable things. I come from a long line of women who walked through fire and I walk today with their fire in my belly. I come from a long line of women who *knew* the long line of women you came from, if not by sight then by *spirit*. And so, to this day, when I see a sister striving in a situation that calls for our ancestors to assemble around our shoulders like a host of heavenly guardians … I silently salute. I *see* you. I *know* you – and you know me too.

THE SUN SETS

The best relationship advice I can give
is to go to bed on an argument sometimes

the sun sets every night and so should you
and every morning when that same sun lights anew
she carries fresh perspectives in her pockets

and whilst you slumber
the moon collects your anger
beaming it up in her mysterious ways
to clear for your new day

leaving only love and space
to find a place of understanding
a softer landing

they work together, those planets and stars
they work hard so you don't have to
let them help you

so you can hold each other more
that's what relationships are for
to remind you that there is no war
here

just someone who wished hard
on lucky charms and shooting stars

to hold you forever near

and to whom you are ever dear.

The fire in your belly
that drives you so
was lit generations
and generations ago.

SACRED PLACE

I don't think love comes and goes
like a bolt from the blue
love is always there, even when you lose
I think love is something you choose
and if you choose someone to give that love to
in sickness and in health
then you'd best be ready to learn a lot about your self
because you will live through so many versions of you
and they will become different people too
and all you need to know
is you can love them as they grow
and learn to let go
love is a choice, and it thrives when given
safe space to voice, your fears
don't ignore your someone's tears
tears are souls connecting
a sign for path correcting
let them wash your face with grace
this love you made, is a truly sacred place.

THE COMPARING

I can tell you why comparison wounds your creativity as deeply as it does. Because your soul is beautiful. When you look at other people's work, the breadth of their talent hits your gloriously open heart like a punch. In the same way that the joys in this life come in such technicolour, they can often feel like pain. And as the wonder of their skills overwhelms your senses, your own shrink away in perspective. Because you cannot for one moment believe that this will happen, exactly the same way, when other people view yours. But it does, my friend, it does. So, the next time someone else's beauty erases all traces of your own, remember this: someone somewhere is looking at something you made and feeling exactly the same. And there is plenty of room, and such *dire need*, for us all to keep creating, exactly as we do.

YELLOW

Some people walk into your life with a light
that can only be described as *yellow*

infusing the very air around with the silent sound
of *this will be okay*
nothing hard can stay
we will find a way
together
we can reach calmer weather

these people, your *yellows*
are sunny, endlessly funny
they are warm and safe
a comforting place

they're a light things can grow in
their heart they wholly throw in
they are cheerleaders for your win

and if you have a *yellow* in this life
keep them bright
they thrive on giving out light
but they fight
their own dark too

they need a colour beside them
to push on through

and I think they found a fellow *yellow*
in you.

BRAVE TO AGE

It is brave to age
in a world which will sell you young

it is brave to embrace
the weathering of your face

in a society that gasps at a wrinkle

it is brave to grey
when we are told the only way

is to hide
those stripes of life

it is brave to save
the worth your learnings gave

and refuse to let the industries buy it
you worked long and hard to acquire it

it is brave to age
to disengage
from the noise
keep your poise

you are magnificent old or new
you are each new version of you
the simple proof you grew
as we are all supposed to do.

OZONE

The ozone layer is healing. Something so vital and so delicate, and so very attacked by our folly, has begun to significantly regenerate. Given space, time, love, the right behaviour and boundaries around itself. Stitching up its wounds in its safe space, rising from the ashes, resurrecting. And I guess what I am trying to say is, if the ozone layer, once so badly impaired, is healing – maybe we can too. And if hope is not within your grasp today and you cannot see a way, perhaps we can ask it how it did this brave thing. And if your day, week, month feels heavy, maybe you can look up there to the sky and smile, knowing it's on the mend now. Knowing it's on its path once more. Knowing, deep down inside, that you will be too. You will be too.

WILDFLOWER

It is a universal truth I'm afraid
that if you grow too high
or glow too bright
there will be those who take it upon themselves
to consume and remove your light

do not let them

a garden without flowers that grew loudly
in soil they were never invited to
would be a sad and colourless place

and truth be told you are far too clever
to let them choose your face
you are not a disgrace
you are a *wildflower*

and they may think themselves tall poppies
sentinels of the soil
but you won't hear them rant or rave
as you wave
your petals to the sunlight
and reach for your share
of all that is your right

wildflower, take your *power*
do not worry about the showers
you grow in rain
it washes shame

that was never yours to claim.

One day you will see
that all of this mud
was simply the soil
that grew you
to full height.

“

Days wasted in the eyes of the
achievers but treasured in
the eyes of the believers.

”

ALL THAT TIME

I want to look back on days filled with cookies and sofa cuddles. Days spent listening to stories I have already heard or helping someone who had lost their way, stay. Days spent counting blessings and laughter and not steps, or grams of protein. Days wasted in the eyes of the achievers but days treasured in the eyes of the believers. I want to look back on the kind of days that feel lit from within, even when it's raining outside and the washing won't dry. Days that just don't need a why. Because I think it is those days that we were supposed to hold dear. And not the ones when our list is cleared. I worry that it will blow our minds when we look back and find, we didn't make the most, of all that precious time.

NIGHTLIGHT

The moon is a nightlight
she exists to guide

and even though her nightly show
is mighty and breathtakingly brilliant
so many resplendent ways she can shine

she doesn't truly wish you to see
no, she wishes you asleep

but if you cannot rest
because you feel not whole
broken hearts and lonely souls
fish lost from their shoals
are her goals

and she knows
how to soothe your fears
and dry your tears
with a simple reminder
that whatever is hurt
she is here

and many more troubled hearts
stare at her glare as you now dare

begging for directions home

the moon is a nightlight
she exists to guide
and she knows

the answer dwells within that well of self

so, she reflects that truth
every night she shows you *you*

and all the *resplendent ways you grew*.

VERY BEST START

Clothes too big, sleeves too long
shoes so new and shiny
photos at doors, backpacks hang
on shoulders that seem so tiny

smiles plastered on, but faces are pale
holding it in with such might
a heart full of love, a lump in your throat
and no sleep for either last night

a world of unrest, a life of unknowns
it's hard to let them be grown
these babies you nurtured with all that you had
feel still too young to be flown

but fly they must and you have to trust
that life will be kind to their heart
a home full of love is what you have made
and you've given
the very best start.

“

It is a thing of great beauty
an ancient duty.

”

THIS PLATONIC SONG

I learned. Many years before. That when my worth is on the floor, much of the romance I need will come from the platonic loves in my life, and not from husband to wife. And that's alright. Because women know. And that is neither excuse nor platitude; it comes from deep gratitude. We understand the neighbourhood, you see. And we thrive, by helping one another survive, this rocky road of hormone-fuelled life. It is a thing of great beauty, an ancient duty. And it is a love I very much rely upon. This platonic song. All along, it has been the grace, that helped me take up much more space.

LOOKING AWAY

I've been looking away
running out of things to say
and the world appears to worsen
with the passing of each new day
I still pray
but I've been looking away

and when I look
I am bone-shook
there is no part of my fragile humanity
that is let off the hook
I am mute

I've been looking away
I've run out of things to say
but I know we cannot grow
if we do not show
our horror
our care
our ability to share
all pain

none of us gain
it is happening again
there is no such thing as *others*
we are all mothers
when children are slain.

TRYING TO BE GOOD

Good people are good people because they are trying to be so. It is not that they are *without* unkind thoughts or critical narrative. It is that they choose to delete the negative and rewrite; with love as the pen and not fear. Everyone filters judgement and criticism daily. It does not make you a bad person. It is what you choose to keep that defines who you are. We cannot control intrusive thoughts thrown out by the ego, but we can control our actions and what we allow out into this world. Good people are not without negativity. They are choosing not to let it lead. They are trying to be good. We are all just trying so hard, every day, to be good. *Trying to bring in moonlight, where darkness would thrive. Trying to choose kindness every moment we're alive.*

A LIFE AROUND

I grew a life around my grief
despite its daunting size
I moved my things to fit it in
and listened when it sighed

I threw my windows open
to bring it nurturing sun
even grief needs daylight
and often craves a little fun

I washed my grief with care
I spoke to it of you
I brought it out to roam the park
the way you'd often do

this grief is quite the lodger
we've fallen into step
we mooch around like soulmates
in work, in play, in rest

and when the days feel light
grief lingers by the door
afraid he can't accompany me
afraid he'll be a bore

but in my heart I make a space
and bring him for the ride
together we walk side by side
I see no need to hide

I grew a life around my grief
I made a home for two
for now this grief's a part of me
the me who's missing you.

ZOOM IN

In a hundred years none of us will be here. We'll all be back to the earth that grew us, or dispersed among the stars which imploded so long ago to give us the building blocks we needed to make this life. And if you have any faith at all in the unexplainable, there we will be. Wondering what all the fuss was about. Wondering why we gave away years of living when we were supposed to use the pain to hyper-focus on the moment. Hyper-focus if you can. Zoom in on the details. Get right up in the face of this gift we are given because it is but a beat in this magical masterpiece. One century out of 45 million so far. Zoom in. Be here. Let go.

THE POSITIVITY PACT

Positivity is misunderstood

it is not the art
of masking emotions

nor is it the practice
of papering over cracks

positive thinking does not work
if you are whitewashing misery
or editing your truth for easier consumption

to become a more positive person
you must make a pact with your inner child
to hear *her* voice above that
of your inner critics and demons

you must promise to allow her to come forth
with her intrinsic belief in your safe passage
through the storms that stir your seas so

positivity is not ignoring negativity
it is *accepting* it
and then choosing to hope for better anyway

it is giving the same weight to the *believing*
as you do to all the *fact*
and in the space between the two
remember your *pact*.

STAR-SHARING FRIEND

Every atom within our bodies
was created long ago in a star
it's *true*
and I like to think that me
and you
were once part of the same star
though it may sound bizarre
you just never seem far
no matter where you are
it is as though we come from
the *same*
and I'll never forget
that feeling when we met
like coming home *again*
not new
oh how I am grateful
you blew
my way in the end
my old
my ever gold
star-sharing friend.

HEAR THEM

If comparison is stopping my creativity, I write about it. If imposter syndrome is cutting off my motivation to pen poetry, I write about that too. If I am too sad to sit down and type, I write about being too sad to sit down and type. And I think you see where I am going. The thing is, there are many emotions in a minute and each of them has the ability to pull you away from what you want, or need, to do. So why not ask them in, involve them. See what they have to say that they must shout so loudly and drown out your focus. Chances are, they just want to be heard, as we all so very much do. So hear them … and carry on.

JOY COMES BACK

When you finally realise

that joy is less fireworks, more firefly
less orchestra, more birdsong

she will come back much more often

for joy will not fight
with the fast pace of this life
she dallies not in the shiny or the new

she breathes in the basic
shimmers in the simple
and dances in the daily to and fro

joy has been beckoning you
for many a year, my friend
you were just too busy doing, to see

the very next time joy wraps
her quiet warmth around you
as the garden embraces
your weary body in its wildness

tip her a nod
you cannot force her to stay
but if you are a gracious host

joy comes back.

“

In all the dust around
your movement, lies the life
you are not seeing.

”

RACING

If you are competing to be the most busy, the most stressed, the most pulled apart at the seams … consider what the prize is here. What trophy is it you work so hard to lay claim to? My friend, in all the dust around your movement, lies the life you are not seeing. The moments you are missing and the stillness you could be ascending towards. There are many podiums to be placed upon in this life, many medals to be collected and proudly worn. Be careful you are racing for the right ones.

STAY

It is hard
to stitch a soul to earth
who doesn't want to stay

and if love was the way
they would all be here today

and perhaps if they were
they would say

give me your guilt
I will cast it astray

I couldn't see
that bright new day
but I pray, you do

all I want now is for you
to push the dark
till light comes through

like you always hoped I'd do.

EXHALE

Breathe out, you are tired
give your worry to the moon
breathe in, be inspired
feel the safety of this room

breathe out, lose your fear
to the coming of the night
breathe in, dawn is near
we embrace the morning light

breathe out, exhale
Mother Nature knows your soul
breathe in, inhale
let her loving make you whole

breathe out, be at ease
with the cycle, with the flow
breathe in, give your load
to the wild to let it go.

To begin something new
you simply need enough
bravery to *begin*
the rest falls
into place.

“

It’s a dark road if you’re travelling in disguise and loaded down with shame.

”

CRACK ON

Crack on with whatever it is you're doing, to bring yourself a sliver of joy in this short life, my friends. Anyone with the time and capacity to judge you, really needs to go and find their own magic. It's a dark road if you're travelling in disguise and loaded down with shame. Be unafraid to shine that quirky light. It will lead the way for so many and free your soul from the box you've been squashed into all this time.

GROWING IN MOONLIGHT

Not many people know
that some things grow, in moonlight

that's right

bravery, for example
does not require sunlight
to grow to full heroic height

it can find its source of power at night

and I think this is evolution
a very simple but clever solution

to getting out of dark spaces
and unsafe places
and as we sleep
our bravery grows deep
ever reaching to reap

ancient power from the moon
her beams assist its bloom
synthesis in midnight gloom

not many people know
that some things grow, in moonlight
at night

as you curl up
small and tight.

STITCHED

I won't be far away
a statement I can wholeheartedly say
because you and I, we are stitched
hitched, by love
it is not something that can be torn
or worn
away
it is the kind of thing
the universe built
to stay

and even when you lay me to sleep
do not ever feel alone when you weep
for my shoulder to cry on, you keep

I am but behind a veil, our love
just as the oceans
will prevail
your tears will sail
to me

to be set free
and returned, kissed by my own
you are never alone
this love
we will always own.

KITE IN THE WIND

The only thing that's linear in this life is time. Everything else loops erratically like a kite in the wind. You don't just heal and move on, life reopens old wounds sometimes, wounds you thought long stitched and soothed. Each time you lose someone or something, you grieve and learn to grow a life around that grief and along comes another tearing which puts you right back in the fog. Nothing is linear except time. Your love will be tested, your wisdom will flourish and then disappear into a murky mindset or a new relationship. Your self-worth will be tight and then it will fly apart at the seams as though it was never once fastened. It is all circles, cycles, speed bumps, mountains and valleys. But when these loops and cycles swoop you up, remember you haven't gone *back*, you're still moving and you're moving *forward*. It's just that this road of infinite infinity you're walking is never straight. Brave heart, deep breaths, and on we loop.

ON TIME

Pray how can it be that you think yourself late
when given a schedule you didn't create
a timeline of busy built solely by man
yet nothing in there was part of your plan

like trees in the forest you grow and you rise
you gather and reach your will to the skies
you age and you yield to the nature around
your roots further delve deeper down in the ground

pray how can you say you have no chapters left
when the book that you're writing is hardly bereft
of adventures and lessons and stories you've woven
as you bravely embrace the choices you've chosen

so hold back their *no's*, their need to restrain
no timeline will stop you from rising again
and again, on and on, you are just learning how
not late, not over, until final bows.

EASILY PLEASED

You have to be easily pleased to enjoy this world,
to thrive amongst its chaos. You have to master the art
of delighting in the ordinary. Learn to revel in the tiny
wins and the moments of peace and see each sunrise
as the opening to a sold-out show. Let the loud stuff,
the tsunami waves, wash themselves out on the rocks,
whilst you paddle in the foam with the sun, or the rain
on your face. Both feel just as good *if you would only
let them.* You have to be easily pleased to enjoy this
world of ours because the wondrousness doesn't shout
above the noise. It babbles like a brook, it breezes
like a spring wind and washes in like breathy waves.
Listen. Look. Be pleased, my friends, be pleased.
There is much to be pleased about.

HAPPY STAY-AT-HOMER

I am a loner
who wants lots of friends
I seek attention
but expect that to end
as soon as I need space
I seek the saving grace of silence
when noise feels like violence

I am a hermit
who needs to see crowds
to experience life when it is loud
but only when my capacity allows

and I think it is alright
to be half day and half night
half peace and half fight
to seek adventure and unfiltered light
to turn to pumpkin
when midnight strikes

I think it is okay
to go wherever
your cellular pathway lays
and to face this life bravely
exactly that way

an often-aloner, a happy stay-at-homer
an occasional roamer.

Positive people aren't ignoring
the darkness of this world
they have dragged themselves
painfully into the light and are
choosing to share it with you.

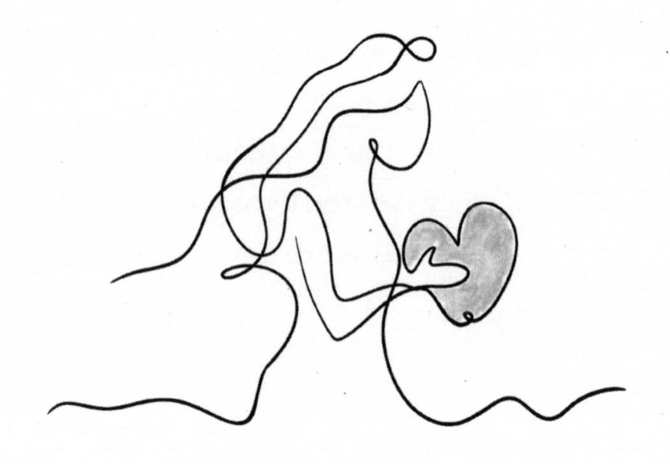

COURAGE TO CREATE

Waking up every day
and choosing love
is *brave*

plucking contentious thoughts
created by the outside seeping in
and replacing them
with home-grown peace
every hour you breathe
takes the strength
of a thousand soldiers

being soft enough
to allow others to be emboldened
by your openness
is to know fear
and face it full-on
every day
square in the eye

like the warrior you are

some may mock
the loveliness in this world
but it took much courage to create.

“

I’m happy with realism
wrapped up in hope.

”

A HOPEFULIST

I'm a former pessimist, a recovering perfectionist, but I'm not aiming for optimism as you may think. I'm happy with realism wrapped up in hope and sprinkled with some 'ah but what if love really *is* the answer'. A *hopefulist* is what I am. I want to see this world for what it is but pull all the bravery I have, out of my boots, and focus my soul vision on helping, and hoping, that things can get better.

MOONBEAMS

We all know about sunbeams, those people who are our rays of sunlight, brilliant and bright. But we never talk about the moonbeams. The people who radiate the kind of ethereal glow that can pull oceans to move and hold planets in place with their magnetism. These lights are often low-key and sometimes unseen but when they move out of your alignment, you can feel that shift of earth and axis. The moonbeams in our lives, the ones who command nature in its very essence, are pillars of knowing, safety, hope and intuition. And something even deeper than that. Something we have not yet named. Look after your moonbeams, for they look after you.

EVERY LITTLE THING

Maybe your life doesn't look
the way you hoped it would
the way you feel it should
but that doesn't mean
your life is not good

squint your eyes
adjust your vision to realise
that all your needs are met
truly, there are no regrets
the loves that you lost
you will never forget
their memory is your safety net

and maybe your life
doesn't look the way you hoped
because the you then
could not cope

with letting go meaning
finding your wings
gaining courage to sing
embracing the joy
that ordinary brings

and how the extraordinary
is actually found
in every, little, thing.

ALL THE MONDAYS

What if we counted all the Mondays lost. All the Mondays given over without a fight to guilt, anxiety and *not being enough*. What if we saw all of those days as a sandy pile in front of our eyes, watching, as our allocated grains shower the bottom of our hourglass at speed. And we realise, too late, that we threw away such *time*. To this false belief that a week is not our own to shape and live through. Somewhere along the way we forgot that Monday is twenty-four hours of opportunity to do more living. Somewhere along the way we handed those days over as a ticket to a life we did not want to go to. Somewhere along the way, we agreed to throw a whole day every week, into a wasteland of worry and fear. I wonder how many Mondays we each have left. I intend to use mine wisely. What about you?

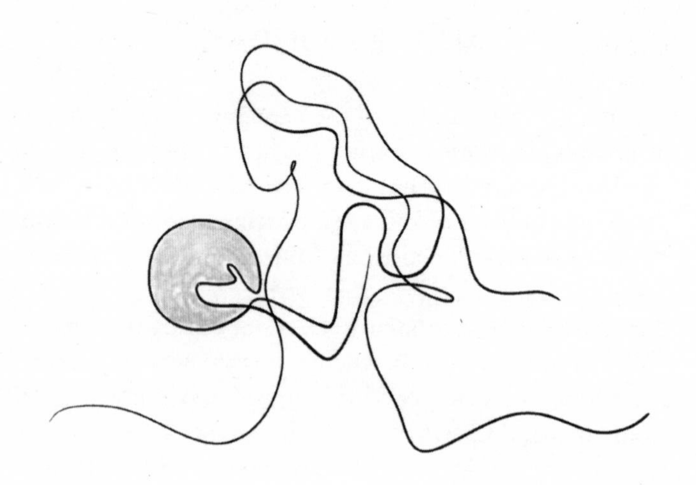

A BRAVER YOU

She asks me is she brave
and I look at her
here
still here
still trying
after all these years

after all the ditches
in which she almost died
all the nights she cracked and cried
a river

am I brave, she quivers
and I show her a mirror

of all the shes
she used to be
and all the ways
she fought to be free

yes I say with the deepest of truth

I have never seen a braver you.

It is brave not to be busy
to be bare and boldly
being when everyone else
strives to buy the
emperor's new clothes.

BUTTER-SIDE DOWN

No one gets away with a life free of time-wasting telephone calls, placed on hold for what feels like an eternity. It is universal: the traffic lights that pop up on the day you most need time on your side, and we all know the slow-motion horror as a fresh piece of toast falls to land butter-side down. I think of how these little snubs connect us; we each get our share. And whilst we know there is much more to be dismayed by, we are human this way, together. I'm sorry if your toast fell butter-side down today but the same gravity and fateful force that brings these things to pass, is also holding us all safely in place. Day in, day out. And isn't that something.

CAME, TO PASS

Perhaps, some relationships
were not supposed to last
perhaps these bonds didn't fail
but simply came, to pass

perhaps, they came to do
exactly what they should
like a rescue plane dropping care
laughter, joy, soul food

and perhaps we ought not fret
that this love we somehow lost
instead we must accept
that missing them was just the cost

perhaps, some relationships
collapse like burning stars
imploding supernova
having stitched a wound to scar

having brought sun to a season
where darkness had a hold
turned confusion into reason
bringing warmth to what was cold

perhaps, some people
were always meant to leave
bringing magic to a place
that had forgotten to believe.

INSIDE A CHILD'S HEART

I'm a sucker for cheesy movies, even the carbon-copy Christmas ones, that make no real sense but feel like the inside of a child's heart. I'm a bringer in of lights, *everywhere*; if I could cover myself I would. I'm a lover of hosting joy, whenever it can be done in this life and making magic of the mundane. Because if people can hate and kill, for no real reason, then I can *love that way too*. And it's hard, this world. It hurts. So if you find your light in anything, take it. Take it, my friends. Let them tell you your passions are silly. I think it's the cleverest thing a human can do ... to remember, what the inside of a child's heart looks like.

GATHER NUTS

I know what it's like to lose hope
to believe that you are not cut out
for this life and its losses
I know what it is like
to be so frozen with fear
that the breath in your lungs becomes brittle
and tears at your broken skin
with every sharply shallow intake

it hurts to breathe
but breathe you must

I know what it is like to be muted
by the myriad ways
in which worry can infest our being
and I know how the cold hard floor
of rock bottom feels

I know the difference
between living
and surviving
and I know that sometimes
we have no choice

but when we do
when we *can* choose living
oh, my friends, please do choose it
I beg this of you

there are chapters in our books
all of our books
that hurt to write and hurt to read

so imprint the joyous
on the inside of your eyelids

paste photo after photo
of the good times there

they will be your drive
when your vision sees nothing
but the despair of your *now*

like the squirrel who gathered nuts all summer
throw yourself into the good days
when they come
and use their fuel
to warm you through the bleak

and hang on
this is living
for all of us

each and every one.

BEAUTY MUTED

The gods of social media
often lead creators
to view an array of shimmering stars
within their field
be inspired, they say
but often, it does not inspire us
it silences us
mutes us into submission
as the skills of other souls
loom shadow over our own

there is too much beauty out there, we fret
why add our own meagre offerings
to this glittering tableau of perfection, we lament
in full imposter dress-up

because if we do not
if any of us do not do our *thing*
perfection may well be what remains

what a travesty that would be

because we know, we *know*

that this world is only beautiful
when imperfection is all around
when in each imperfect artwork
someone's breathtaking is found.

“

Let your apologies be something they are familiar with and not desperately seeking of.

”

LET THEM SEE

Let your children see you sit, without supplying reason for your idle. Let them understand it is perfectly okay to just *be*. Then let them see you busy too, but busy doing joyful things sometimes, just *because*. Let them see you confused, unsure, sorry. Let your apologies be something they are familiar with and not desperately seeking of. Let your children see you access all the colours of life's spectrum. So they may grow knowing a human is never just a handful of things but rather a unique slice of absolutely everything. A universe in skin. Sun, moon and stars with fingers, toes, eyes and ears. Let your children *see* you. So they may *know* you. And know themselves too.

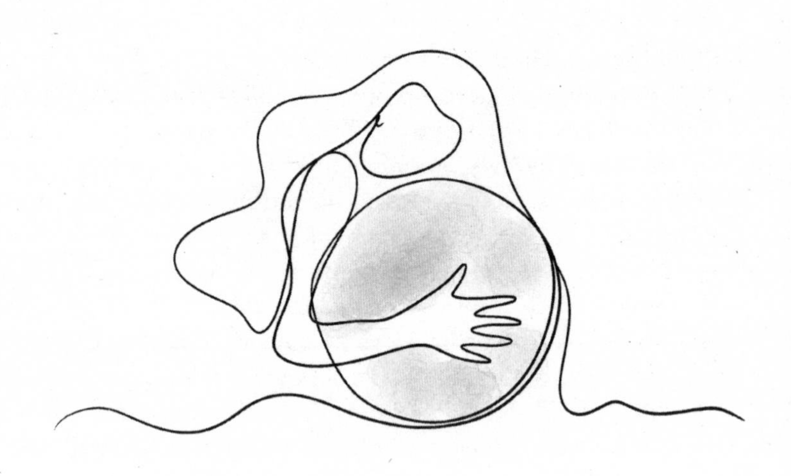

SEEDS

Everyone has a mantra
a phrase they repeat when courage is required
perhaps they heard those words on the radio
read it in a book
or maybe it was said by you?
it may surprise you to know
you are the voice in someone's mind
from time to time
that something you relayed
has become another's *way*
maybe you can recall
whose voice it is that you play?
I wonder if they know
how far their words can up and go?
everyone has a mantra
and I think, perhaps
everyone has gifted a mantra too
imagine if we all knew
those seeds of strength we grew.

She's so sensitive

they say

that's my favourite thing

about her

I reply.

YOU CROSSED MY MIND

I was just about to send you a little video of two friends giggling as one stumbled. They could barely breathe through uncontrollable snorts and giddy, joyous tears. It made me belly-laugh just the way I do when you and I are together. But like life itself, my feed quickly moved on and I was distracted, by something not quite so time-wastingly wonderful. So, I thought I would simply send you the message contained within this little moment instead:

I love the very bones of your soul.

“

The you who lives with that person *inside*, not *out*.

”

A PIECE OF THEIR SOUL

You lose a version of yourself when a loved one leaves. But you will eventually greet a new version of yourself too, when the daze dissipates. The you who lives with that person *inside*, not *out*. The you who claims a part of them, as a vital new part of you. The you who continues to shine their light into this world so it doesn't feel their loss quite as much. The you who is only really you because they were them. And so you ensure they carry on existing. The you who takes their love, their light, their passion, and channels it into all you do from this moment onwards. You lose a version of you when someone special leaves, but I think you also gain a tiny piece of their soul, to carry safely back home to them. Until you meet again.

A NEW VERSION OF YOU

In times when you do not feel like your old self
I think it is because you are not
you are changing, again

a new version of you is coming
to accept the baton from the old

you are changing guard
but unlike the ceremonial soldiers
this doesn't happen swiftly

it's more like a butterfly
emerging from a cocoon
having dissolved to sticky residue
ready to reform
ready to break through the shell
you built yourself without realising

you feel your wings
tapping at the surface
itching to unfurl
but not yet sure of their strength

and something in your soul is reminding you
that the only way to know
if these wings are ready to hold your weight
is to go to the edge and try them out

put faith in your process, in nature's process

a time of change is coming for you
and so whilst you make the final tweaks
to this next version
take a moment to look at the old ones
talk to them, forgive them,
apologise to them
put them at peace
remind them
they were exactly
as they were supposed to be

remind them
we will see many more versions
before the final one holds us all
and takes us home.

SAVE YOURSELF

You don't have to save everyone
the worry of this world
is not yours to bear
you only have to save yourself

and I don't know how
but that *doing* will spread
it will call out in echoes
like whale song through waters
it will whisper in hopeless ears
that someone somewhere
saved their soul today

and a heart that had laid down
in defeat, will beat
faster, with hope
like you threw someone a rope

you don't have to save everyone
but save yourself
and the magic of this magnetic rock
will take care of the rest.

CHOOSE YOUR SCARY

I have to constantly remind myself
I am worthy
I have to consistently fend off
imposter syndrome
apathy and fear

when I wake each day
I am almost immediately attacked
by my inner critic
who sees my journey between
the world of sleep and waking
as vulnerability
a chance to cut me off
at the starting block of the day

I am growing still, every day
reprogramming, learning, seeking
failing, floundering and flawed

I often wish I could go back
to the old me
masked and hidden
safe in the shadows

but going back is not an option
when you start this journey to self
and staying the same
is no way to use this life of ours

we only get one

but we do get to experience that one life
as many versions of ourselves
and that is exciting

we can see this world from all perspectives
by the time we are through
if we choose

yes, we only get one life
but we are given many chances
to live it differently

it takes bravery
it is scary
but not doing it
not seizing each chance to evolve
is much scarier to me

I guess what I am trying to say
in a roundabout way is
choose your *scary*
some will free you
some will cage you
let you be you
or enslave you

this life can be terrifyingly
exhilaratingly, exhaustingly immersive

if you are doing it right.

Boundaries are not walls
they are intricate fences of
invisible golden thread that
filter all things toxic but
let love and light through.

“

I think our loved ones direct the flow of energy around us.

”

ORCHESTRA

Our passed loved ones send us signs, this we know. But I also think they send other people. I think they whisper in ears as those strangers sleep and somehow bring them our way; a new friend, a much-needed confidante, bountiful bringers of joy to help you as you heal the wounds which cannot truly ever heal – but can definitely be *looked after*. I think our loved ones direct the flow of energy around us, like a conductor with their orchestra. Making sweet music for your life. Creating soundtracks of happenings to hug you in their honour. Watch out for their work, my friends. I think it's beautiful. And I think it's happening right here, right now.

WINDS OF CHANGE

A wind of change blew in last night
rattling window frames
reminding all who felt its blast
that nothing stays the same

this gale whipped up a frenzy
an air of dread and fear
it swooped up all the status quo
and dropped it far from here

it tore apart my comfort zone
which took me time and toil
it whisked away my safety net
and razed my home to soil

as the new dawn spread its light
across this barren scene
it hurt to breathe the fresh new air
so fearful I have been

but winds of change don't fly alone
they travel in a crowd
the knowing from our ancestors
their instincts, screaming loud

the memories of past times we flew
when ground was whipped away
our wings that caught us many times
grow stronger every day

and winds of change bring bright new light
and keys to unlock doors
that hide our vast reserves of strength
when we need to find some more

so let it go, flow with the wind
don't face against her power
these winds they know, to move, is life
that's how a garden flowers

take time to settle, like the seeds
that soar around the air
your time to rise comes soon enough
dig deep, you will get there.

BORROW YOUR BRAVE

You let me borrow your brave again
my courageous, heart-holding
soul-keeping friend

you hid me with your shield
when the crossfire saw me yield
sat with me on the floor
when my legs could hold no more

you gave me ammunition
defended my position
smoothed the path
for my transition

again
stood with me until the end
what strength I found in such a friend

as you

one day, you may
borrow my brave too

the brave that came from loving you.

LOOKING FOR SOMETHING BEAUTIFUL

People who first discovered gems, diamonds or gold, must have been searching pretty hard for something beautiful. Gems encased in rock look like rock. And gold must be scoured for, over and over, sifting through gravel and soil for days on end, endless toil often without the grace of that shine. The first time, in everything, comes without the added comfort of the *knowing*, so therefore must be fuelled by the *hope*; that magic is always around, that if this earth can host so much beauty, surely there is no end to that vault? I guess what I am trying to say is, if you are always looking for something beautiful, you have far more chance of finding it, than those who simply walk over rocks, seeing only rocks.

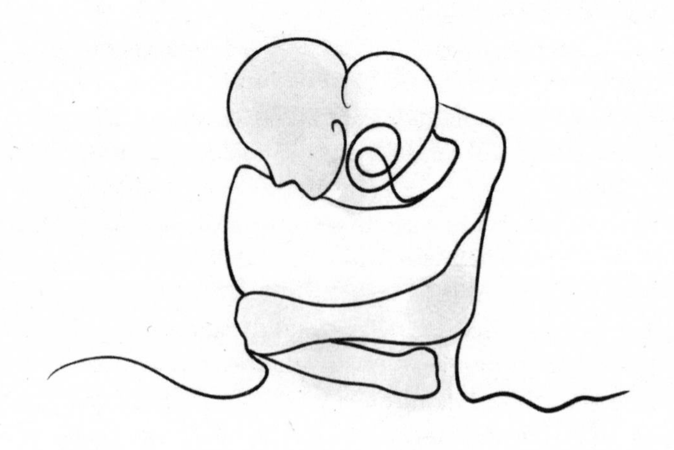

LEFT YOU NOT

If you cannot live without me, do not

let sleep lead you to that mysterious soil
that bridge between heaven and this mortal coil
where faith is the way and facts simply spoil

I'll meet you there

we will walk and I will show you
that I still see you, I still know you
and that just like you, I grow too

here
away from worry and fear
I carry you ever near

and the robins bring my news your way
and sing me back the things you say

if you cannot bear the world
without me

do not
let death be forgot
for I have left you not.

THE UNEXPECTED FRIEND

New friends who simply appear in your life, are without doubt gifts from Mother Nature. Just as the beloved grandparent from your formative years would slip a rolled-up note into your hand as you left; *a little something just for you, dear*. These meet-cutes, which ease themselves into our story without pomp or ceremony, are the surprise money in our hands we so very much needed but did not expect. If you find yourself with such a treasure, hold it tight, my friends. Something wonderful has crossed your palm. These unexpected friendships are the magic. *Let them in*.

The magnificence of the moon
is rarely captured by camera
what makes you think
you are any different?

SPECIAL

If you love a child who is special
in the way their brain maps out
then chances are you know
what *tiger* love is all about

the need to fight their corner
when they're up against that wall
the instinct of the *mother*
can make you twelve feet tall

you'll understand the surge of love
from deep within your soul
when that little fighter smashes
another hard-won goal

this world can feel quite frightening
as you watch them leave your door
your heart within your mouth
your stomach flat upon the floor

if you love a child so different
who the world can't understand
then you'll know the joyous moments
when they truly learn to stand

your pride is off the scale
your love a wondrous thing
I'm glad you know the special light
that *special* children bring.

INNER CHILD

Your inner child is not sitting pretty in a bow-tied dress with polished shoes. No, she is a fighter, that one. She has dirt on her face, grass in her hair and is ready to jump in water and throw caution to the wind at any given moment. She is driven purely by hope, that child, and her heart is lion-sized and mighty. She does not care for your talk of *pretty* or *graceful*, she cares for the breeze in her hair and the sun on her face. Your inner child is the voice that pushes you to say *yes* more, but only to the good stuff. Let her say yes today. Let her play. She has waited patiently enough. And patience is not her best virtue.

WISH YOU COURAGE

I wish you courage
to release and let go
of limits that choke
your magical flow

I wish you courage
to end and renew
create bright new versions
but always, core *you*

I wish you courage
to fail many times
knowing that victory
lives outside those lines

I wish you courage
to crave warm and soft
to brave being kind
wave that proudly aloft

I wish you courage
to channel your pain
like fuel it will kickstart
your joy once again

I wish you courage
to love what is gone
to see through the veil
to believe we live on

I wish you courage
to use the word no
without need to explain
let its meaning be so

I wish you courage
to cease to compare
as with flowering fields
each deserves to be there

I wish you courage
to hammer it home
that a life cannot thrive
on *achievements* alone

I wish you courage
to peer into beyond
to acknowledge your gifts
before they are gone

I wish you courage
in a someone who fights
for your soul, for your heart
a connection so right

I wish you courage
to create that bond too
the thrill of a life
where *you* showed up for *you*

I wish you courage
to go back to the wild
to rebuild the bridge
to your lost inner child

I wish you courage
to welcome the new
not a thing's truly lost
if you know where to view.

ASK THE OCEAN

If you wish to hurt me
you will find that task easy
I am a sitting target
as soft as fresh snow
and as delicate as a dandelion seed
if you wish to hurt me you will do so
and it may satisfy the unhealed pain in you
to see me weep
but I am so very used to hurting
in this everything world of ours
that I do it like the ocean
roused to rage by storm and gale
I thrash and I roar, I rise and I crash
and with the dawning of a new day
and a softer breeze
I let go and melt to the shore
I do not let each hurt make me harder
I have no time for becoming brittle
when everyone knows (ask the ocean)
that soft is where the strength lives.

ALGORITHMS

When the comments do not come
when there are no likes
when your square is lost and lonely
you are still so very bright

your value does not sway
with the reels they play
or don't, or won't

you cannot be boxed
just open these locks
let your truth set the value
of your stocks

face the sun, sweet child
they will come
we are all *someone*
and anyway

this was supposed to be fun.

LET'S TALK

Let's talk, you and I
let's get to the core
if we wade through the pain
it won't hurt any more

let's examine those things
we were told not to say
so they'd fester inside
rotting more with each day

let's dig for the deep stuff
let's throw it all out
there's nothing to hide
let your inner child shout

let's talk, you and I
let's unstitch the past
so light can take leave
of the darkness, at last

and fresh air will flow
through the veins of your heart
let's talk till the beat
of your new life restarts

let's channel our ancestors
down on their knees
and claim what is theirs
the dreams they believed

let's carry the flags
of the passion they grew
and mix with our own
till their vision holds true

let's talk and keep talking
don't fret who you'll shock
each word is a key
let them open the locks.

Shake fear and ask it *will this kill me*?
Because yes, breaking hurts
but living a life of suffocating safety
hurts harder than that.

SHOW AND TELL

I think social media can be beautiful, actually. So many people, showing up every day, bringing something that is just ever so *them*. There we all are, reading one another's posts, feeling inspired, informed, supported or seen, and then creating one of our own to do the same for someone else. It's like show and tell for adulthood. *This is what makes my spirit light*, we say. *Come look at what I created from my heart*, we say ... *This lifted my soul and I wanted to lift yours too*, we say. I think it can be wonderful, actually. Keep showing up to show and tell. Keep *telling*. It's uniting, it brings community. And we all need a bit more of that.

YOUR UGLY

Show me your ugly
the parts you hide away
I will not even flinch

I'll stay

show me your ugly
the rage you ram within
let it meet with my acceptance

I'll win

show me your ugly
the scars you cannot bear
I will look at them as beauty does

I'll stare

show me your ugly
I will show my ugly too
and together we will make
that ugly

something new.

“

A great teacher sprinkles this
world with their magic as the
children they teach rise up
and fly so far.

”

A GREAT TEACHER

A great teacher is a human with a soft heart, who bravely commits to letting hundreds of even softer hearts into theirs, to be held safe. A great teacher is a watering can, daily nursing seeds so precious, they never stop scanning the sky for hawks and lightning. A great teacher keeps their garden safe and secure but also a little wild and free, teaching those seeds to bloom in any soil no matter the surrounding and reminding them they are not crops, they are all the flowers this earth proudly hosts. A great teacher sleeps with little faces on their minds and delicate self-worths nestling safely in their soul. A great teacher sprinkles this world with their magic as the children they teach rise up and fly so far. And does all of this around their own life. If you know a teacher like this, water their soil sometimes too. They give their own away so freely.

WITH ALL THAT WILDNESS

I hope my daughter is beautiful
in the wildest of ways
like tree roots
reaching deep into the earth, fierce, not *cute*

and growing as deeply as her branches will rise
reaching to the beckoning skies
and down into the core, always aware
there is *more*

I hope my daughter is free
like sea foam must be
a product of oceans commanded by moon
finding space where there was no room
and riding life as it is cresting
flying, finding, creating, nesting

I hope my daughter is beautiful
in the way that wind is not dutiful
conducting the garden to bend and sway
and knowing the only possible way
is to join that dance

and be blown as you blow
it's how she'll grow
I hope she will know

that beauty is like fire and ice
it rarely thrives in sweet or nice
but rather of the dusty ground

in which her growing place is found

I hope my daughter's beauty bound
with all that wildness swirling round.

SHE SENT

She sent me a book
with a page turned down
I barely had strength to read it
but I knew with my knowing
that she also knew
there was something in there
my heart needed

and as I began to take the words in
tears found their way to my cheeks
the lump in my throat let forth a soft howl
I'd been keeping inside for some weeks

like floodgates thrown open
a storm was released
a bottled-up genie set free
all of the magic I'd kept trapped inside
and all of those versions of me

she sent me a book
with a corner turned down
she sent me a key to my cage
all of her love and all of my pain
let loose
with the turn of a page.

BRUISE

Finding a new garden in which to grow to full splendour is hard. But staying in barren soil will slowly kill you from the roots up. Taking a leap of faith requires a core of steel, but so does allowing your dreams to go out like a used match. Speaking your truth will make your knees knock and your voice tremble, but holding it in is an oil slick in a coral reef. Living life unmasked will leave you open, but that mask is cutting off your oxygen at the source, my love. The thing is, living is hard, but dying slowly is *hard too*. You will bruise reaching out of your comfort zone and you will rot staying inside it. This life, it will wound you every day and stitch you right back up again, if you are living it right. None of it is easy. Choose your bruise.

THE MEANING OF LIFE

The meaning of life?

to me, is clear
that the reason for all of it
the *why we are here*
is everything
the fingerprints only you can bring
the way your growth
aligns with spring
and retreats to beat
with winter

each of us a sparkling splinter
of universe
unique and diverse
yet of the same
we all gather to play this game
then forget why we came

and I blame thinking
when we should be linking
fingers together
and arms around trees
not letting the rat race
bring us to our knees
we seek *peace*, a sweet *release*

but we look in wrong places
we search for traces
of ourselves
in bottomless wells

such tales we tell
of heaven and hell

but I think they exist in our hearts
perhaps not worlds apart
after all

the meaning of life?

it is *all*

in the small.

The people who make you
feel you are too much
do so because they feel
they're not enough.

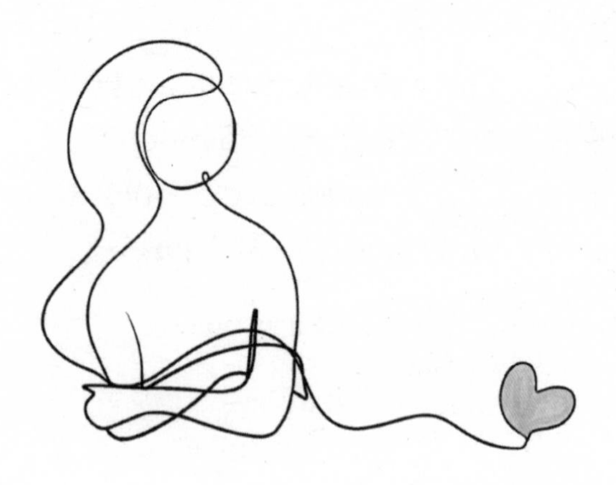

GRIEF IS NOT A PLACE

Grief is a not a place to stay
walk away
but let it walk in step beside you

grief is not a home to nest in
or rest in

it is a shadow to be found
when the sunlight hits the ground
stitched to your foot
it will take root
a favourite chapter in your book

reminding you that you are now more
than you were before
because you store, someone's love

not less, because they left

you're still you
but with that part of them attached too

together you go on
it is the same song

just with new notes

notes, their leaving
wrote.

COURAGE STEPS OUT

Courage does not charge in confidently
on a fiery steed dripping
with dare-do and valour

courage simply steps out of the shadows
where she tirelessly and continuously
toils behind the scenes
also afraid

and when her time to rise comes
courage clears her throat
pushes shoulders back
breathes deeply to steady
the tremble in her voice
and calls upon faith, knowing
and ancient intuition
to flank her sides for fight

courage is not always confident
but she *knows*
that if she is defeated in the battle
she will win the war

because she found out long ago
that being knocked down
is not something to fear
but being too scared to break
very much is.

COFFEE WITH THE UNIVERSE

I took a moment today
let the grind slip away
and thought of all the loving things
I so very rarely say
(lord let me change those lonely ways)

I watched a mother feed her son
and an older lady gazing at everyone
like they had stories worth sharing
her energy so curiously caring
(forgive me for soul-staring)

I sent some texts that were in my heart
some of them I had already partly written
I allowed my broken heart to be smitten

with the hugeness of my little life
all the ways I could be lost to strife

my coffee today was, a lot
a universe saying forget me not
(stop and look at all you have got).

“

To feel that you belong, you must decide that you do.

”

BELONG

Fitting in and belonging are not the same energy. You can't feel as though you belong anywhere, until you make a home for yourself in your own soul. A place where you are safe – whether flawed, achieving or in stasis. Fitting in is the ego's desire to be like the rest, to move with the crowd. It is fuelled by the unhealed parts we weren't taught to nurture early on. But it's never too late. To feel that you belong, you must decide that you do. Accept yourself through your own front door and make a home for life. You'll never feel the urge to fit in again, if you belong, at home, within yourself.

BRAVERY LIVES

Bravery lives in the way we love
despite loss being the only possible outcome

bravery lives in allowing stories to unfold
as they will
being brave enough not to sell yourself
to someone who is unconvinced of your worth

bravery is in the learning
to fight your battles within
instead of outwith
as long as all your *yous* are united
let them say and do what they will
with their perception of your character
only you can know the truth there
and that is your power to protect
it takes bravery to do so

bravery is continually reaching for sunlight
when someone is covering you with shade
and knowing your worth is not theirs to decide

bravery is identifying what is fear
and what is life
will it kill you
will it harm someone
or is it scary because it is *living*
and we have learned to survive?

whisper *brave* to yourself
when you need to be still
when you need to be loud
and when you need to show up, again

whisper brave to yourself
when you give yourself permission to rest
to break, or to leave

whisper brave to yourself
before you sleep, upon waking
and each time
that unexpected feeling of hope
flutters into your heart
it is brave to allow it, you see

you've been burned before
and you'll be burned, again
but all that *living* in between
will make the heat
so very much worth it.

If there is a secret
to unlocking a wonderful life
it is to be fearless enough
to take pleasure from the
simple every day.

TELL THE OTHERS

If you have tasted contentment
by learning to let go of perfection
tell the others

if you have found peace
by learning to avoid drama and chaos
tell the others

if you have understood the mission
that we are here to thrive, not succeed
tell the others

whatever lessons you are learning
whatever lightbulb moments you experience
tell anyone
who cares to listen

each *tell*
is a pebble skipped into a lake
making ripples

and ripples can build a new life
or even save one about to go under.

WILL BE BRAVE

Let girls be brave by clearing their throats
and speaking the words their grandmothers wrote
let boys be brave by questioning why
society wishes their eyes wouldn't cry

let women be brave by seizing their rights
to be safe on the streets as they walk home at night
let men be brave by loving their soft
by flying it high, waving proudly aloft

let people be brave by remaining unique
by looking within for the lead that they seek
by throwing aside the masks we are given
then stepping outside, authentic and driven

let humans be brave by seeing the light
by claiming the wrongs of the past to put right
by loving this planet we each walk upon
and loving each other whatever our song

let hearts be brave by saying goodbye
and knowing this circle is why we're alive
by grabbing the grief and squeezing it tight
till love comes cascading out of its might

let souls be brave by loving again
even though we all know there's one way it can end
let love be the reason, the why and the way
let love be your life and your life will be brave.

FOREVER DAYS

There will be days that stick to the inside of your mind forever. Days that refuse to be forgotten, no matter what. And I think this is because these were days we got just right. This living. When we balanced the busyness with love. When we were present in body and spirit. Days when we reached out to invite others and reached in to invite ourselves too. Days when laughter and tears were both just as welcome and joy and sadness held hands beneath the table. Days where not much happened but actually, everything did. There will be days that become forever days, and they don't announce their arrival in advance, but at some point you will feel a sense of utter contentment wash through your bones and dust your skin with goosebumps … and that's when your soul takes a snapshot, and hangs it on the pinboard of your mind. To be gazed upon with fondness, forevermore.

GROWING BRAVE

I've been growing my brave
in a little pot on the windowsill
I stand close and very still
and whisper sweet nothings in its ear
I know it can hear

I shower it with hope and feed its soil
with an ancient knowing
that life is always flowing
that bravery is not simply showing, your teeth
sometimes it is having the courage, to believe
the strength, to grieve

I've been growing my brave
its cuttings I save, pressed flat on a page
they serve as a reminder
that bravery, requires you to be kinder
and it is beautiful, this thing I grew
using all I ever knew

I hope you can grow your brave too
go out there, just you
being gloriously, vulnerably true
proud of all the ways you grew
as you were always supposed to do.

AFTERWORD

If you saw yourself within these pages, welcome. There are many of us out there, braving to be bare, shedding old coats we no longer need and seeking out better ways to exist in this world of ours. Come and join us on social media if you are not there already. We remind one another daily that bravery does not always bray in the bravado; sometimes it barely whispers in the wilderness. Yet brave it is. And if you have found yours, at all, I am proud of you. And on we go, together …

ACKNOWLEDGEMENTS

First thanks, as always, goes to my followers. Whenever I have shared faced fears and been honest with them about my nerves or disarray, they have received me with a safety net of solidarity and sisterhood. It emboldens me no end. At my first launch event, when physical symptoms held me back, I was able to share it with them and their effusive acceptance of me just as I am brought in immediate relief and courage. They literally held me up.

As always, love and respect to my husband and family who create such a solid base at home so I may fly here and there sometimes; it is never taken for granted.

And to my editor, Susanna, and the team at Black & White Publishing/Bonnier Books UK, especially Flora, Kevin, Lucy, Ella and Nick, for their unwavering enthusiasm and ongoing embrace. Never feels like work!

Finally, whilst we are here being thankful, I would love to take a moment, you and I, to thank ourselves. It is a lot, this life. This world is a lot. And we deal with so much on a daily basis. It can be missed in a flurry of fuss, failure and fanfare. I think it's vital that we stop sometimes and look at who we are and how much we have faced, endured, survived and come through. You are always growing, my friend, and you are brave in ways you cannot always see. I hope this helped clear your vision a little. There is much bravery there to behold.

ABOUT THE AUTHOR

Donna Ashworth is a No. 1 *Sunday Times* bestselling poet. She lives in the hills of Scotland with her husband, two sons, Brian and Dave (the dogs) and Sheldon (the cat).

Donna started her social media accounts in 2018 in a bid to create a safe social space for women to come together and connect, but her love of all things wordy quickly became the focus and a past love for poetry was reignited. Over nine books and 1.8 million followers later, Donna is delighted daily with her mission to shower the world with words and make poetry a go-to in our wellbeing toolkit.

'I believe wholeheartedly in the power of opening a daily poetry page to better everyone's mental health and clear space within our minds. Poetry is permission to feel everything we as humans are absolutely supposed to, knowing we are not alone, *never* alone. Poetry is not folly for the fancy; it is using words to shift perspectives, heal wounds and let in light again. And it is something we can pass to one another when times become turbulent, as they so often will.'

Facebook @DonnaAshworth
Instagram @DonnaAshworthWords
TikTok @DonnaAshworthWordy
X @Donna_Ashworth

AUDIO

If you have enjoyed these pages and are someone who practises meditation or uses affirmations and music to relax and reset, my collections are also available as audio books. Perhaps you can dip in and out when driving or listen along whilst walking in nature; the perfect pairing. However you chose to use my words, I am simply delighted you do at all. Thank you, enjoy and, hopefully, speak soon.